KT-116-139

Watching Grizzly Bears in North America

Elizabeth Miles

Heinemann
LIBRARY

www.heinemann.co.uk/library
Visit our website to find out more information about Heinemann Library books.

To order:

   Phone 44 (0) 1865 888066

   Send a fax to 44 (0) 1865 314091

   Visit the Heinemann Bookshop at www.heinemann.co.uk/library to browse our catalogue
and order online.

First published in Great Britain by Heinemann Library,
Halley Court, Jordan Hill, Oxford OX2 8EJ, part of
Harcourt Education. Heinemann is a registered
trademark of Harcourt Education Ltd.

© Harcourt Education Ltd 2006
The moral right of the proprietor has been asserted.

All rights reserved. No part of this publication may be
reproduced, stored in a retrieval system, or
transmitted in any form or by any means, electronic,
mechanical, photocopying, recording, or otherwise,
without either the prior written permission of the
Publishers or a licence permitting restricted copying in
the United Kingdom issued by the Copyright Licensing
Agency Ltd, 90 Tottenham Court Road, London W1T 4LP
(www.cla.co.uk).

Editorial: Nancy Dickmann and Sarah Chappelow
Design: Ron Kamen and edesign
Illustrations: Martin Sanders
Picture Research: Maria Joannou and
Christine Martin
Production: Camilla Crask
Originated by Modern Age
Printed and bound in Italy by Printer Trento srl

ISBN 0 431 19069 0
10 09 08 07 06
10 9 8 7 6 5 4 3 2 1

British Library Cataloguing in Publication Data
Miles, Elizabeth
Watching grizzly bears in North America. – (Wild world)
599.7'8417
A full catalogue record for this book is available from the
British Library.

Acknowledgements
The Publishers would like to thank the following for
permission to reproduce the following photographs:
Alamy pp. 25 (Curtis Richter), 28 (Franzfoto.com); Ardea
pp. 13 (M Watson), 20 (Jean Michel Labat); Corbis pp. 4
(Kennan Ward), 18 (Joe McDonald), 29 (Kennan Ward);
Creatas pp. 5 (bottom), 26, 28; FLPA pp. 8 (Michio
Hoshino), 22 (L Lee Rue), 27 (Michio Hoshino); Getty
Images pp. 9, 14, 17; KPT Power Photos p. 7; NHPA pp. 5
(top T Kitchin & T Hurst), 10 (John Shaw), 12 (Rich
Kirchner); PhotoLibrary.com pp. 15 (Konrad Wothe), 23
(Daniel Cox); Science Photo Library p. 11 (William Ervin);
Still Pictures p. 19 (Ted Miller); Zefa p. 16 (E & B Bauer);
Steve Bloom p. 24. Cover photograph of grizzly bears
reproduced with permission of Nature Picture Library/Eric
Baccega.

The publishers would like to thank Michael Bright of
the BBC Natural History Unit for his assistance in the
preparation of this book.

Every effort has been made to contact copyright holders
of any material reproduced in this book. Any omissions
will be rectified in subsequent printings if notice is given to
the publishers. The paper used to print this book comes
from sustainable resources.

Contents

Words written in bold, **like this**, are explained in the glossary.

Meet the grizzlies

This is North America, home of the grizzly bears. Grizzly bears are big brown bears. Bears are strong **mammals** with thick, long fur.

▼ *Some grizzly bears have hairs with white tips that make their fur look grizzled (grey).*

There are nine kinds of bear. They come in different colours and sizes. Grizzly bears, or grizzlies, are the only kind to have a **hump** on their shoulders.

Black bears (above) and polar bears (left) are two other kinds of bear.

Where do grizzly bears live?

North America is a large **continent** with many different types of land. There are deserts, forests, mountains, and valleys. Grizzlies live in mountains and forests.

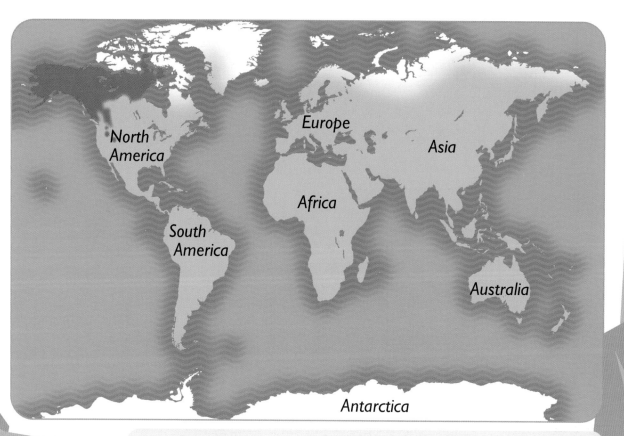

North America

Europe

Asia

Africa

South America

Australia

Antarctica

Key ● This colour shows where grizzly bears live in North America.

Rivers and streams run down the mountains and hills.

In the mountain areas of North America, there are forests and **meadows**. Lots of trees, bushes, and grasses grow here. Many animals live here, too.

There's a bear!

Grizzlies are not easy to find. Their brown fur makes them hard to see against the land. This grizzly is walking on its four large feet on the grass.

▼ *The **hump** on this bear's shoulders tells you it is a grizzly bear.*

42 teeth

small round ears

A grizzly bear's claws are twice as long as your finger.

strong paws

long claws

thick fur

Grizzlies are very large and strong. They must be watched from a safe distance! A large grizzly weighs about the same as six grown-up people.

Bear territory

Most grizzlies like to live alone. They each have a **territory**. It can be as big as a large city. **Male** grizzlies usually stay in the same territory all their life.

▲ *This grizzly's territory covers **meadows**, woodlands, hills, and streams.*

A male grizzly will fight any other bears that come into its territory. **Female** grizzlies make sure their **cubs** do not wander into male territories.

🔺 *The grizzly rubs its **scent** on a tree to warn other bears to keep away.*

Woodland food

Grizzlies eat grasses, roots, and animals. In spring, there are many young animals in the woods. The grizzly can kill a young deer with its strong paws.

▶▶ *Instead of killing animals to eat, grizzlies sometimes prefer to find and eat* **carrion**.

In spring and summer there are lots of **insects** to eat. The grizzly tears the bark off trees with its sharp claws. It can eat the insects hiding underneath.

▶▶ *This grizzly is looking for a meal in this tree.*

Fast or slow?

Grizzlies may look too big to move fast, but they can run faster than you. A grizzly runs as fast as a car to catch a young deer.

▶▶ *It is hard to escape from a running grizzly.*

In spring, fish called salmon **migrate** up the rivers of North America. A grizzly is quick enough to grab a jumping fish with its big front paws.

▲ *This grizzly stands in the river ready to grab its food.*

Mating

In early summer the grizzlies get together to **mate**. A **male** grizzly walks up to a **female**. It takes time for the female to accept him.

▲ *At first, the female grizzly tries to frighten the male away.*

The female bear is much smaller than the male.

The male stays with the female for two weeks. Afterwards, the female is **pregnant**. Her **cubs** will not be born until winter comes.

In the heat

In summer, grizzlies shed some of their thick fur, but they still get hot in the sun. On hot days they will lie in the **shade** to keep cool.

▲ *In mid-summer, the grizzly will go up hills or mountains to find fresh grasses.*

In the summer, grizzlies spend most of their time eating. This grizzly can smell a mouse. It scratches at the ground to get the mouse out of its underground nest.

The grizzly uses its sharp, curved claws to dig.

Winter is coming

In the autumn, the grizzlies get ready for the cold winter ahead. They eat lots of berries to build up their strength. Each bear digs a winter **den**.

▲ *The grizzly digs its den under a tree because the tree roots make the roof strong.*

When winter comes there are few berries left. The grasses are covered in snow. It is time for the grizzly to go into its den to sleep.

The grizzly stays in the den for the winter and is asleep most of the time.

In the den

After a few months, the **female** grizzly has her **cubs**. The cubs are born in the dark, warm **den**. Outside, it is still snowy and cold.

▲ **Newborn** *cubs have little fur and they cannot see or hear.*

The cubs stay in the den and drink their mother's milk. After two months the cubs have grown bigger. The den gets crowded.

⮝ *These cubs are not yet old enough to leave the den.*

Young cubs

In the spring the weather is warmer. The young **cubs** leave the **den** for the first time. They are three months old.

▼ *To be safe, the young cubs stay close to their mother.*

By spring, the cubs are eating the same kind of food as their mother. The cubs play-fight together. This teaches them how to protect themselves.

▽ *Cubs watch their mother. They learn how to find berries and* **insects** *to eat.*

Grizzlies in danger

Cubs stay close to their mother for safety. If they wander away, **male** bears or wolves might hunt and kill them.

▶▶ *A wolf can easily catch a bear cub. The cubs cannot run very fast.*

In a few years, the cubs have learnt everything they need to know from their mother. They are stronger now. It is time for the cubs to begin life on their own.

Each young bear sets off to find its own **territory**.

Tracker's guide

When you want to watch animals in the wild, you need to find them first. You can look for clues they leave behind.

A grizzly's paw print shows five toes with long claws.

◀◀ Grizzlies leave holes behind where they have been digging for food.

▶▶ Sometimes grizzlies leave scratch marks high on a tree.

Glossary

carrion animals that have already died or been killed by another animal

continent the world is split into seven large areas of land called continents. Each continent is divided into different countries.

cub young grizzly bear

den bear's home, often under ground or in a cave

female animal that can become a mother when it is grown up. Girls and women are female people.

hump lump on the back

insect small animal with six legs and three main parts to its body. Ants, beetles, and bees are all insects.

male animal that can become a father when it is grown up. Boys and men are male people.

mammal group of animals that feed their babies their own milk and have some hair on their bodies

mate when male and female animals produce young

meadow area where grasses and flowers grow

migrate travel a long distance, following the same journey every year

newborn just been born

pregnant when a female has mated with a male and young are growing inside her

scent smell left by an animal

shade cooler places hidden from the sun by things such as trees or grasses

territory area where an animal lives and feeds

Find out more

Books

Continents: North America, M. Fox (Heinemann Library, 2002)

Mountain Explorer, Greg Pyers (Raintree, 2004)

Why am I a Mammal? Greg Pyers (Raintree, 2005)

Websites

Find out more amazing facts about grizzly bears at:
http://www.nationalgeographic.com/kids/creature_feature/0010/index.html

Look at this website for more information about these creatures:
http://www.kidsplanet.org/factsheets/grizzly_bear.html

Disclaimer

All the internet addresses (URLs) given in this book were valid at the time of going to press. However, due to the dynamic nature of the internet, some addresses may have changed, or sites may have ceased to exist since publication. While the author and publishers regret any inconvenience this may cause readers, no responsibility for such changes can be accepted by either the author(s) or the publishers.

Index

Titles in the *Wild World* series include:

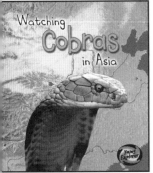
Hardback   0 431 19066 6

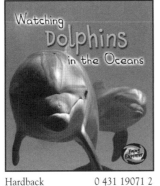
Hardback   0 431 19071 2

Hardback   0 431 19084 4

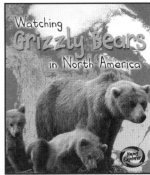
Hardback   0 431 19069 0

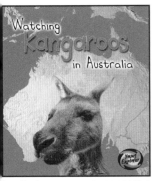

Hardback   0 431 19067 4

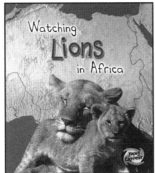

Hardback   0 431 19064 X

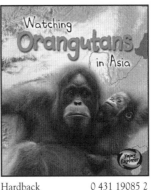
Hardback   0 431 19085 2

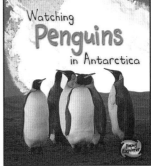
Hardback   0 431 19065 8

Hardback   0 431 19068 2

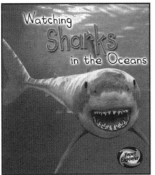
Hardback   0 431 19086 0

Hardback   0 431 19070 4

Find out about other Heinemann Library titles on our website www.heinemann.co.uk/library